GREAT LITTLE BOOK
OF

LET'S DO
DOTS and MAZES

Published by Playmore Inc., Publishers 230 Fifth Avenue, New York, N.Y. 10001 and Waldman Publishing Corp., 570 Seventh Avenue, New York, N.Y. 10018

Printed in Canada

THREE
There are more than three ways to get trapped!

Native Name Game

I have a mane and tail like a horse and a head like a cow. Some people call me a wildebeest. Connect the dots below to find my native name.

FOLLOW THE DOTS to find out who is hooting!

3-D MAZE
This one will make you dizzy!

ICEBERG
Don't smack into them!

CANYON CRAZE!
Don't get lost!

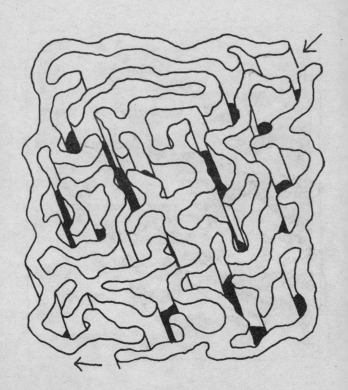

A CUP THAT RUNS OVER
Can you wiggle your way through?

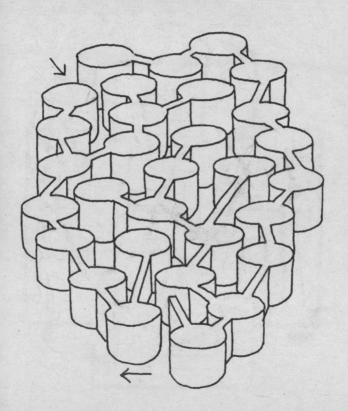

AERIAL VIEW
A toughie to figure out!

ONE-EYED MONSTER
He can still see you! Can you slip by?

FOLLOW THE DOTS to see who is fun to hug!

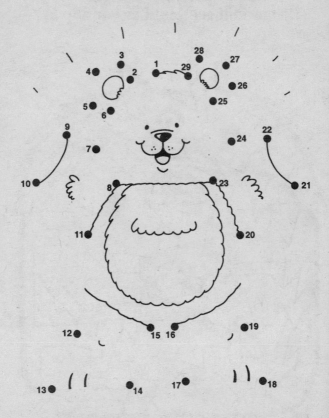

WITCH TIME!
Don't let her get you!

FOLLOW THE DOTS to meet a goofy monster!

CREATURE TIME
Start at the mane and see if you can get out!

FOLLOW THE DOTS to see who's at the beach today!

MONSTER BILL
Monster Bill says there's no escape!

FOLLOW THE DOTS to see what burns brightly during Christmas!

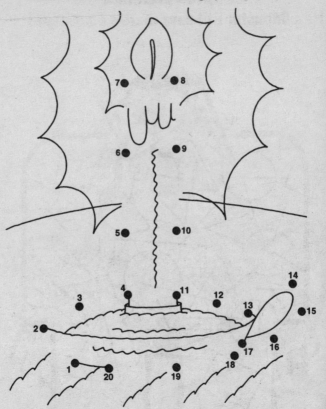

GHOST CATCHER
He's behind the plate and out to get you! Find your way out!

FOLLOW THE DOTS to see a great shape bubble!

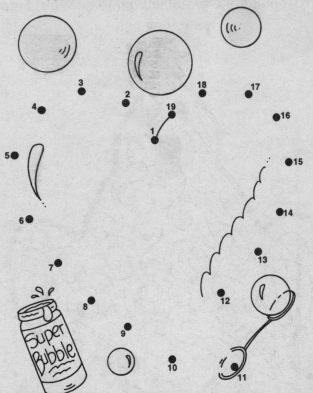

WACKY WALDO
Can you slip past him?

FOLLOW THE DOTS to see what candy comes in!

GHOUL'S DELIGHT
Not just another pretty face!

SEVEN
It takes more than a lucky number to solve this one!

FOLLOW THE DOTS to see a carved message!

FOLLOW THE DOTS to find Santa's helper!

SCARY HARRY
You're smart enough to outwit him!

FISH FACE
Don't go the wrong way!

FOLLOW THE DOTS to see who says "Ho, Ho, Ho!"

FOLLOW THE DOTS to see who loves mud!

GUS GOBLIN
Can you find the right path?

FOLLOW THE DOTS to see where honey is made!

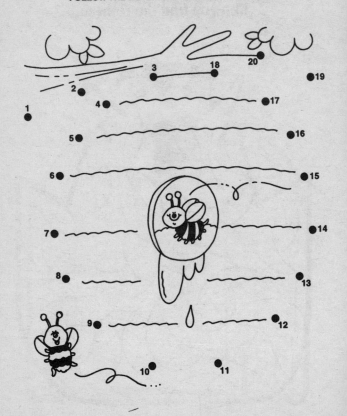

GORILLA
Swing through this one!

GHOST
Swirl you way out of this trap!

THE FIG MAZE
It's tough to fig-ure out!

WATERMELON MAZE
Can you slip through the seeds?

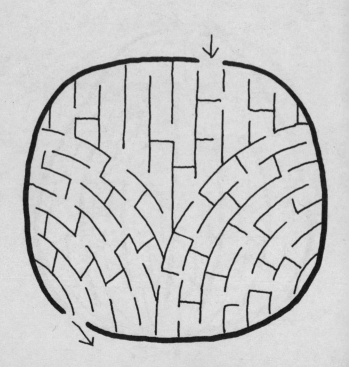

GRAPEFRUIT MAZE
Here's a healthy test for your skills!

PEACH MAZE
A juicy problem to solve!

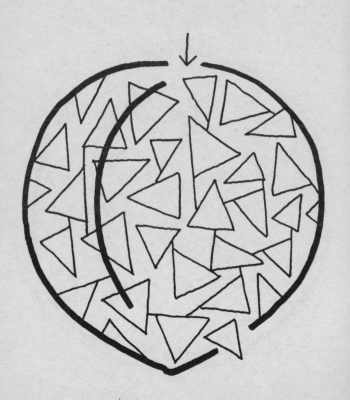

ORANGE MAZE
Peel your way through this one!

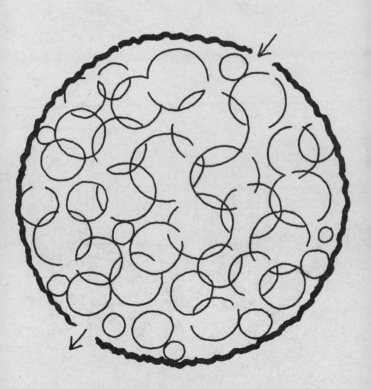

FOLLOW THE DOTS to see what brings circus animals to town!

LEMON MAZE
Don't let this one turn you sour!

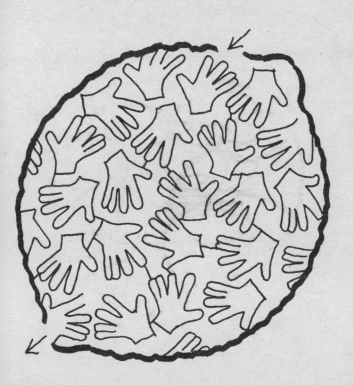

FOLLOW THE DOTS to see what flies high in the clouds!

ONE
There's only one way out!

STRAWBERRY MAZE
Can you patch your way out of here!

AVOCADO MAZE
This one will turn you green!

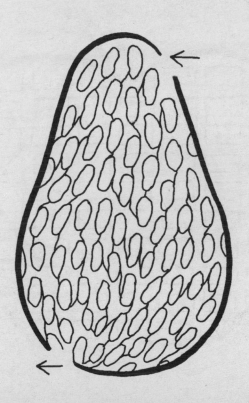

APPLE MAZE
An apple maze a day will drive you crazy!

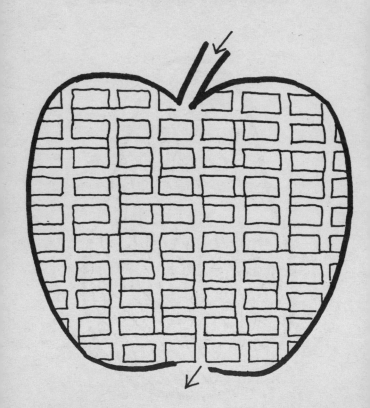

CACTUS MAZE
You have to be sharp to do this one!

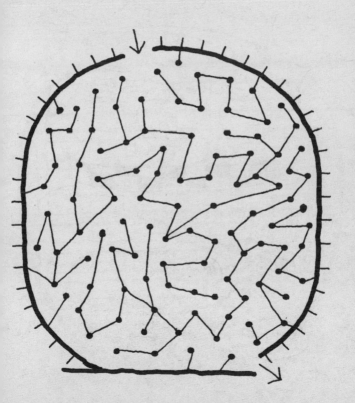

FOLLOW THE DOTS to see where cookies are kept!

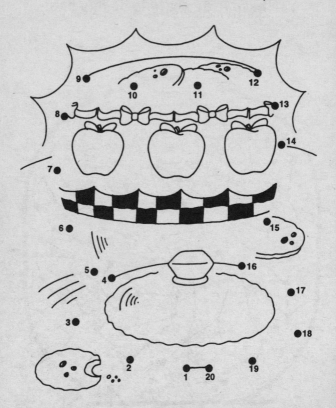

FOLLOW THE DOTS to find a halloween friend!

FOLLOW THE DOTS to see who wants
to make a batch of Halloween brew!

IGGY PIGGY
This one brings home the bacon!

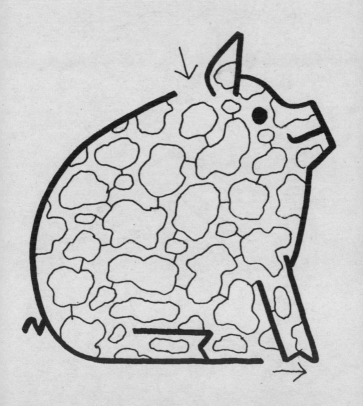

FOLLOW THE DOTS to see who howls at the Halloween moon!

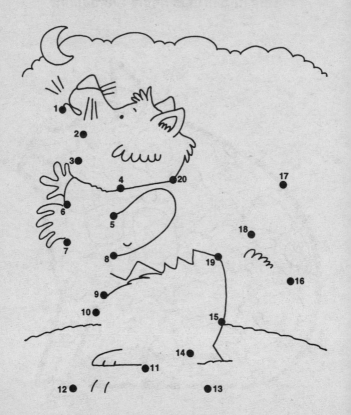

FOLLOW THE DOTS to see what blasts into outer space!

ROADRUNNER MAZE
This maze belongs to the swift!

BUFFALO MAZE
Stampede your way through!

BIRD IN THE SKY
Wing your way through this baby!

FOLLOW THE DOTS to see who lives in the corn field!

FOLLOW THE DOTS to see what was cut out!

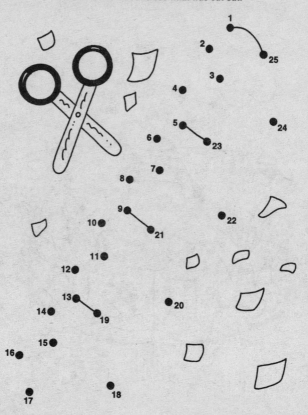

GRUMPY GOAT
You have to be stubborn to find the path!

FOLLOW THE DOTS to see what Shannon is wearing for a costume!

CREEPY CRAWLER
Inch your way through!

TOAD TIME
Look before you leap!

SLUG
Can you slug your way in and out?

FOLLOW THE DOTS to find something creepy crawly!

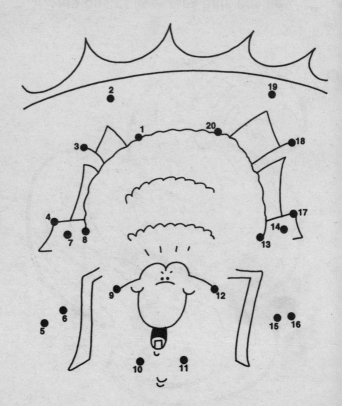

RAPID RABBIT
Hop on down the maze!

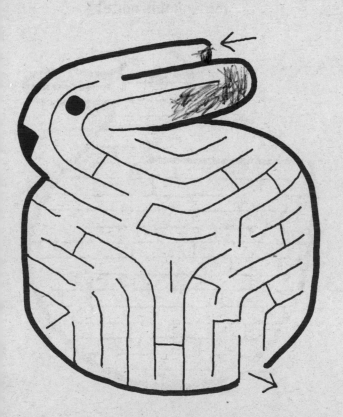

LUCKY DUCK
It will take some luck to get through this maze!

CHICKEN
Not me! I can solve it!

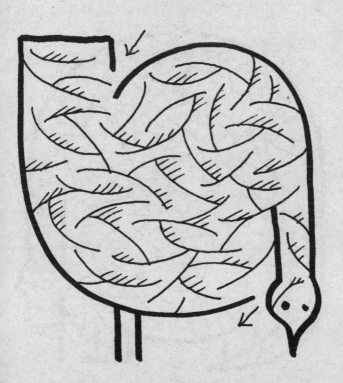

DINO MAZE
Climb out before you become extinct!

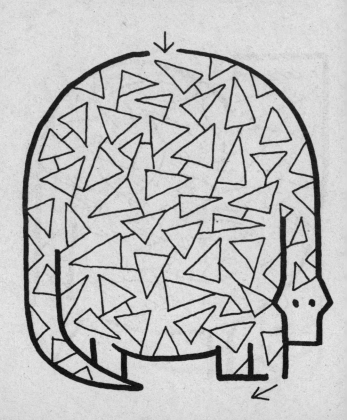

ON YOUR BELLY
Can you snake your way through?

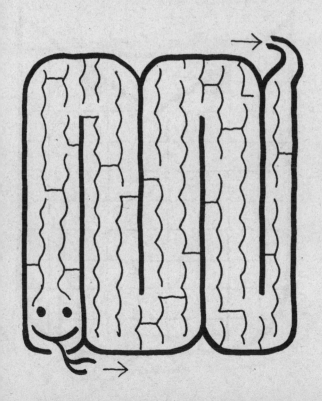

OWL FUN
Are you wise enough to figure it out?

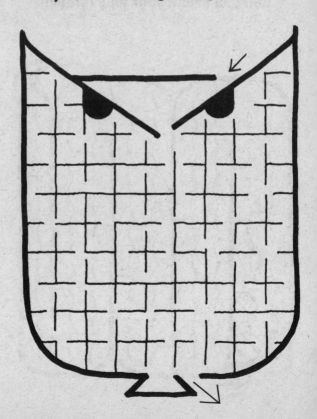

GEORGIA
Here's a peach of a maze.

OPOSSUM
Can you play this one?

WILD BOAR
You'll get a charge out of this maze!

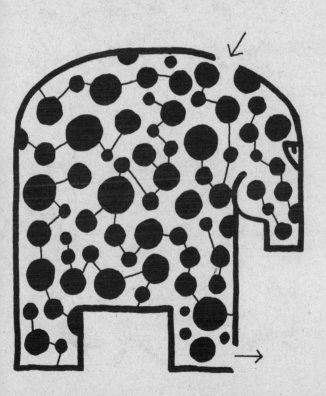

FOLLOW THE DOTS to find a good place to paint a picture!

FOLLOW THE DOTS to see where farm animals live!

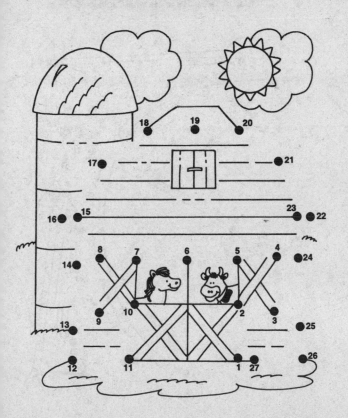

FOLLOW THE DOTS to see what Cupid uses!

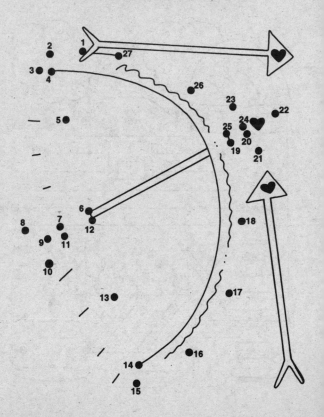

CAT MAZE
Here's the purr-fect challenge!

VULTURE
Swoop in and out!

ELEPHANT TIME
Tramp your way through!

GULL MAZE
Don't be gulled by this one!

WHALE
It will take a whale of an effort to get out!

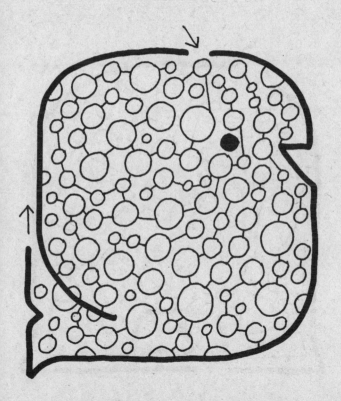

TURTLE TIME
It's the old shell game!

MARINE MAMMAL
Swim on down!

FOLLOW THE DOTS to see where baby birds live!

PORGY MAZE
In one way and out the other!

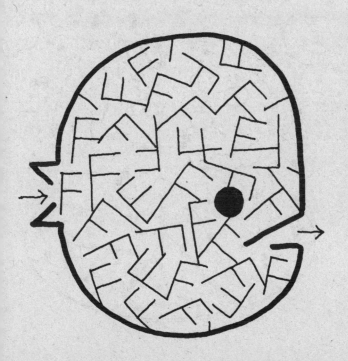

FOLLOW THE DOTS to find a yummy Valentine's Day dessert!

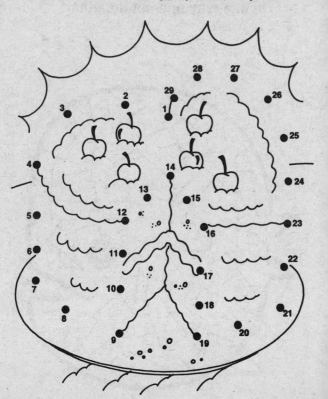

TWO
Does it take two of you to find the right path?

BIRD HOUSE
Help the bird find his way out!

FOLLOW THE DOTS to see what this dog is getting!

FLOWER POT
Dig your way down!

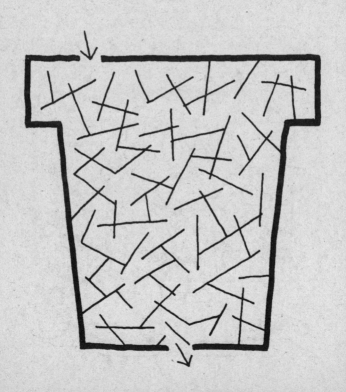

BARREL MAZE
More fun than a barrel of monkeys.

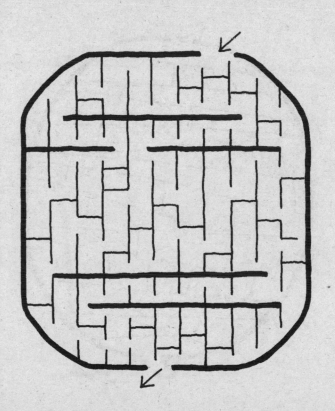

BALLOON MAZE
Float on through!

FOLLOW THE DOTS to see what hangs on your door for the holiday!

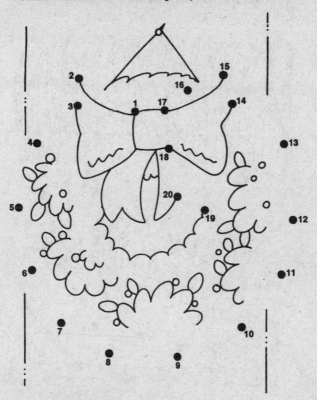

FOLLOW THE DOTS to see who is on the move!

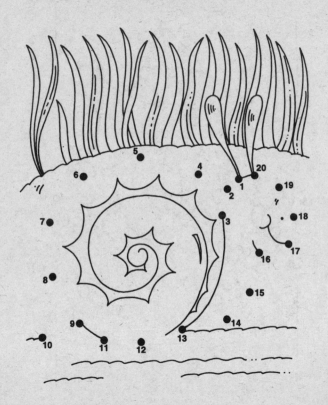

CHERRY TREE
Can you find your way out the trunk?

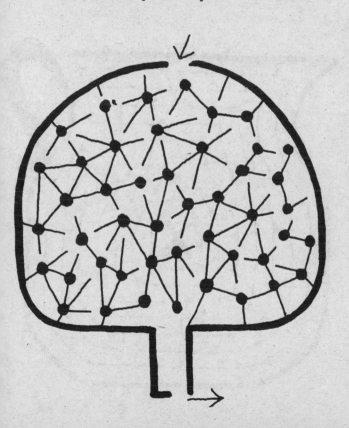

PITCHER OF PUZZLES
X marks the spot!

CHIMNEY MAZE
It should be a clean sweep!

FOLLOW THE DOTS to see who is spouting "Hello!"

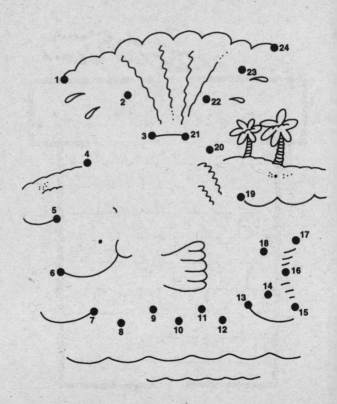

FOLLOW THE DOTS to see delicious Christmas goodies!

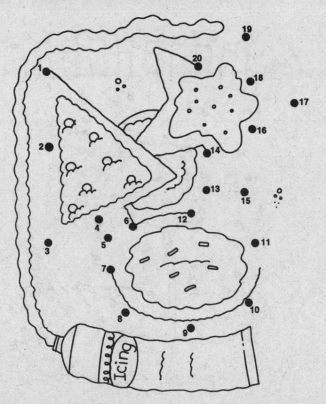

FOLLOW THE DOTS to see what's growing in the garden!

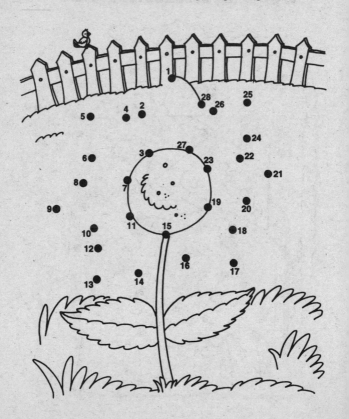

PICTURE FRAME
A work of art!

BARNYARD SCRAMBLE
Can you make hay with this maze!

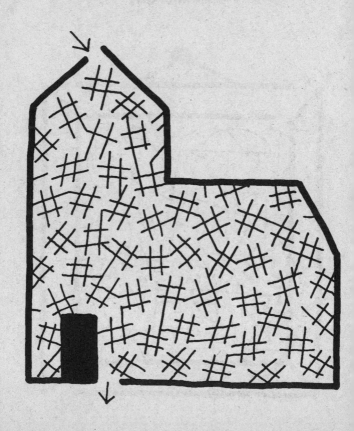

FOOTBALL HELMET
This is a tough one to tackle!

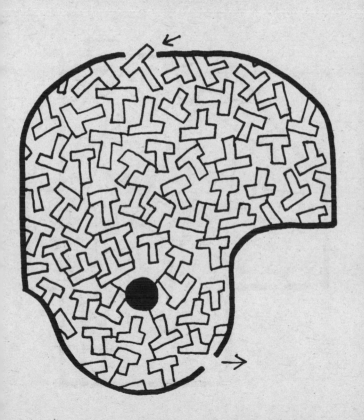

FOUR
If the little fours don't get you, the big one will!

CUBE
This one will box you in!

TULIP
Tiptoe through the maze!

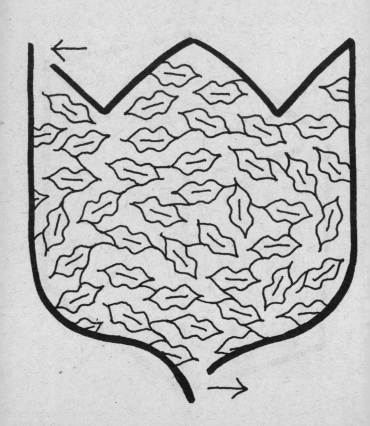

BOOT
This is a maze you'll get a kick out of!

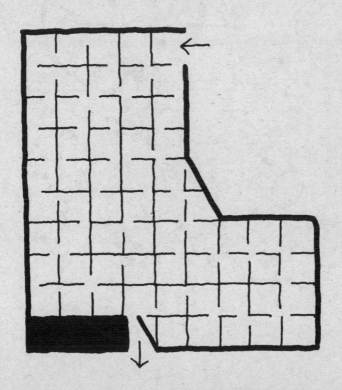

FOLLOW THE DOTS to see what we hang on the Christmas Tree!

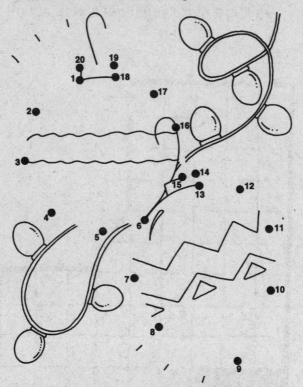

THOSE LIPS!
Kiss this one good-bye!

COLORADO
Can you find your way through the Rockies?

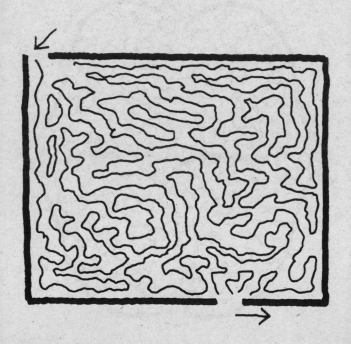

FOLLOW THE DOTS to see what Chad dressed up as for halloween!

IN THE TREE
Find your way in and out of this birdhouse!

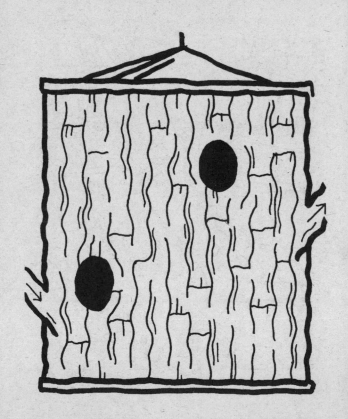

SHIELD MAZE
This maze offers no protection!

**FOLLOW THE DOTS to see who's trick or treating
at Frankenstein's house!**

FOLLOW THE DOTS to find a frosty friend!

CROSSWORD
A puzzle of a maze!

FOLLOW THE DOTS to see what's made out of gingerbread!

BIRD HOUSE BAFFLER
Here's an even trickier one for you!

ROMAN HELMET
Only a maze gladiator can solve it!

Follow the Dots

To discover the national animal of Canada, the largest deer in the world!

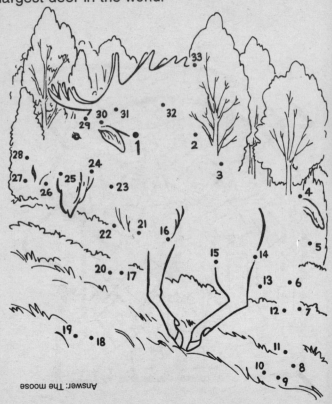

TEN
Now you've just done ten mystifying mazes. But there's lots more to come!

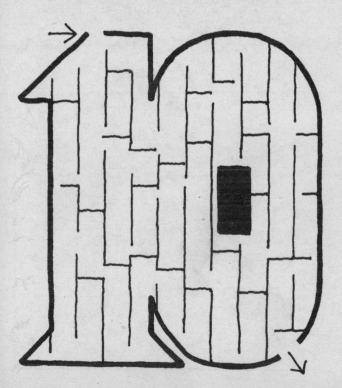

Follow the Dots

Discover what animal climbs high cliffs for safety.

Answer: Big horn sheep

ARKANSAS
Even a President would have trouble with this one!

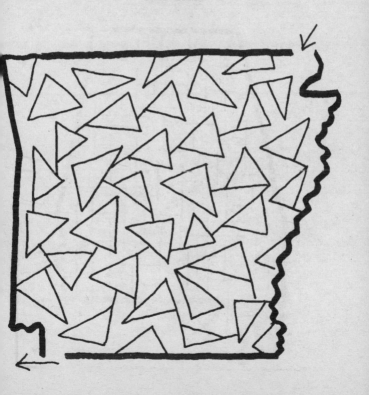

ALABAMA
Can you make it through, or are you just whistling Dixie?

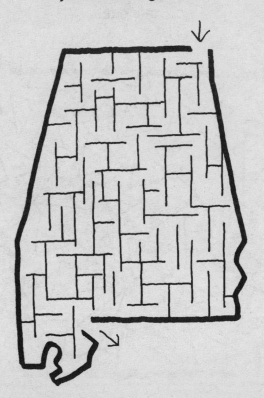

Follow the Dots

Find an animal that uses its odor for protection.

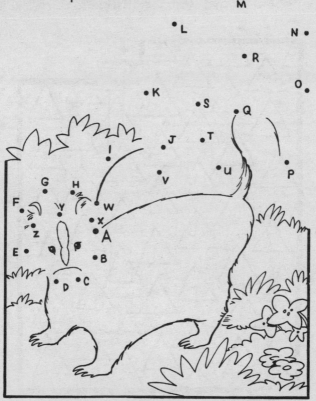

UTAH
Ski down this tricky maze!

Follow the Dots

Discover an animal whose name means "Earth Pig." His thick hide protects him from termites.

Answer: Aardvark

Follow the Dots

To see an animal that lives in the cold far North. His thick coat helps him withstand frigid weather.

OHIO
Can you slip through these letters?

Follow the Dots
Find a hiding
Spider Monkey,
who lives in
trees.

MISSOURI
Show me! you can solve this one.

FIVE
Give yourself at least five chances to solve this one!

Follow the Dots

Find an **indri,** a primate that lives in trees.

ICE MAZE
Keep moving, keep warm! It's cold in there!

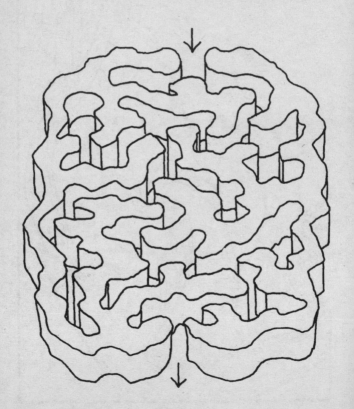

FOLLOW THE DOTS to see what this Valentine's Day message is on!

TEXAS
Hats off to you for finding the right way!

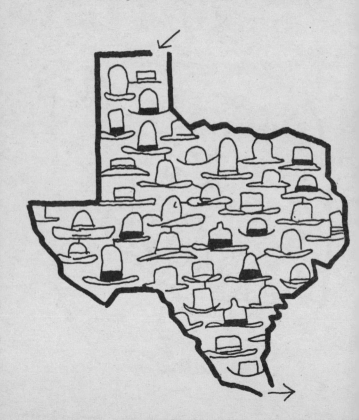

SIX
You'll need a six-shooter to blast your way through!

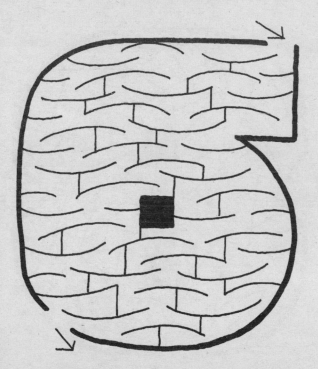

EIGHT
More turns than a figure eight to find your way out!

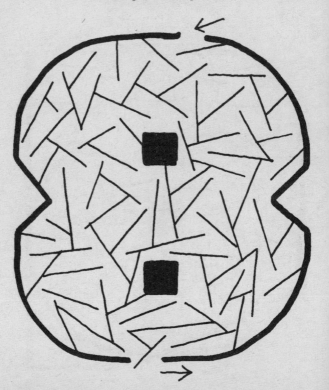

ARIZONA
You have to be sharp to get through the cacti!

Follow the Dots

Discover an exotic bird that lives deep in the jungle, eating fruit from the trees.

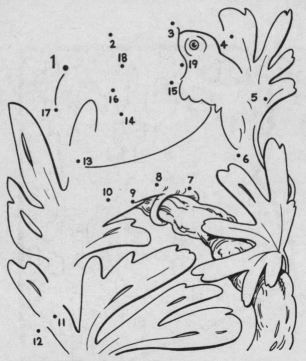

Follow the Dots

See an animal who has 4 stomachs to digest grass and is kept by man for her milk and her meat.

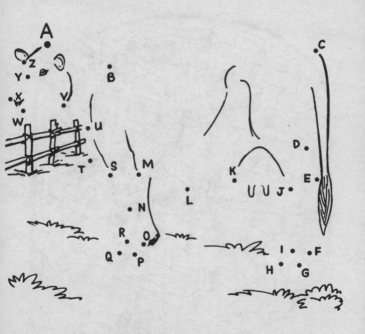

CORRIDOR CHAOS
Can you find your way through the offices?

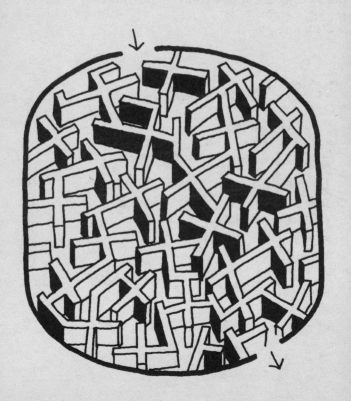

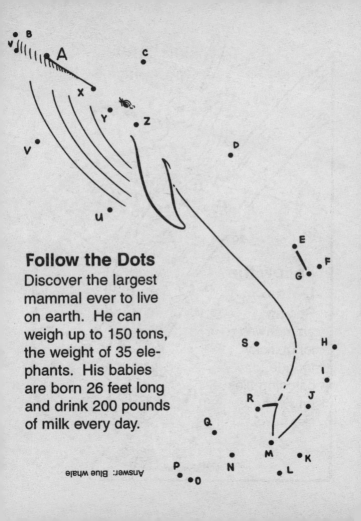

Follow the Dots

Discover the largest mammal ever to live on earth. He can weigh up to 150 tons, the weight of 35 elephants. His babies are born 26 feet long and drink 200 pounds of milk every day.

Answer: Blue whale

Follow the Dots

See an animal with a long sticky tongue for catching flies and mitten-like paws.

Answer: Chameleon

Follow the Dots

To find a **slow loris.** He is active at night and sleeps during the day.

FOLLOW THE DOTS to see who's floating on an iceberg!

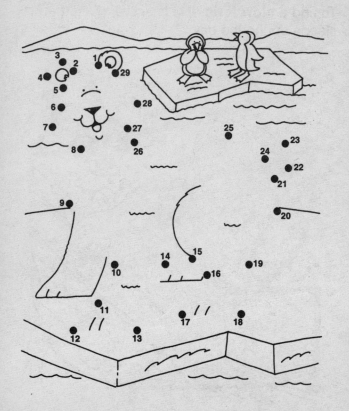

NINE
You'll be on cloud nine when you solve this!

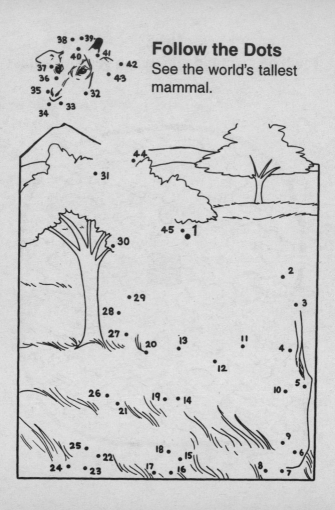

Follow the Dots
See the world's tallest mammal.

FOLLOW THE DOTS to see what you can get at the Ice Cream truck!

LOUISIANA
This maze will really swamp you!

FOLLOW THE DOTS to see a jack-o'-lantern!

Follow the Dots

Find the only marsupial who lives in America. He forages at night and when frightened "plays dead."

RAVINE HUNTER
Can you slip through the cracks?

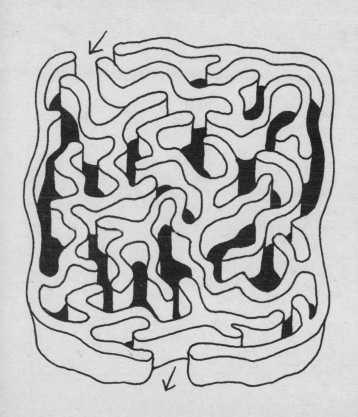

FOLLOW THE DOTS to find out who has lots of legs!

BARBED WIRE
Don't get stuck on it!

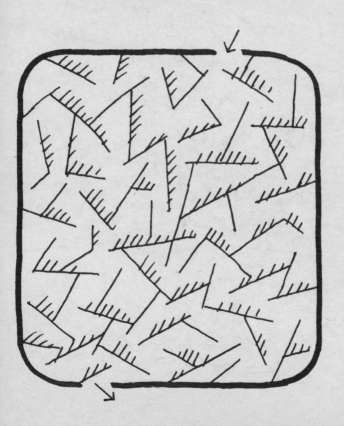

FOLLOW THE DOTS to meet a goofy monster!

WATER DROPLET
Slide your way through!

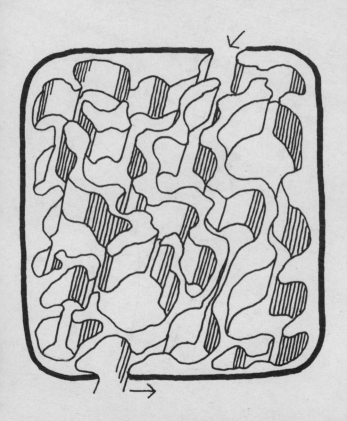

FOLLOW THE DOTS to see what Santa fills!

**FOLLOW THE DOTS to see what toad thinks
the witch should add to her brew!**

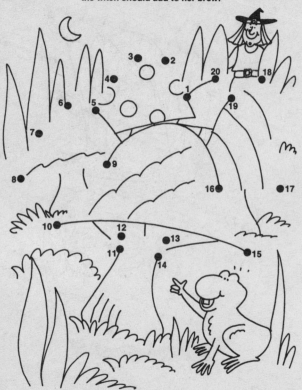

FOLLOW THE DOTS to see sweet treats!

FOLLOW THE DOTS to see what the kids built in the tree!

FOLLOW THE DOTS to find out what people give to trick or treaters!

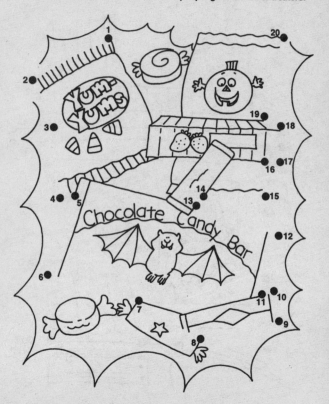

FOLLOW THE DOTS to find a Valentine's drink!

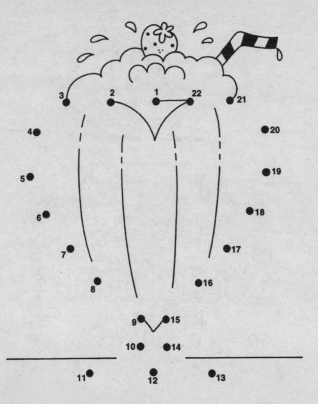

FOLLOW THE DOTS to see a place to put Valentines!

FOLLOW THE DOTS to see a Valentine's day visitor!

FOLLOW THE DOTS to see who has beautiful wings!

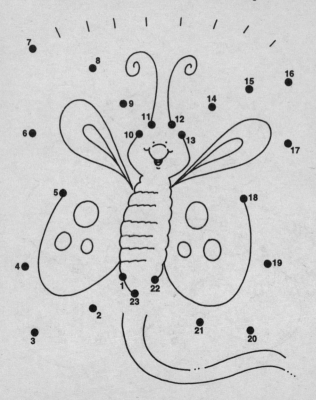

FOLLOW THE DOTS to see what the witch will make her brew in!

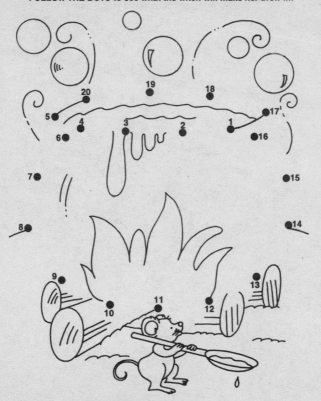

FOLLOW THE DOTS to see the witch's pet!

FOLLOW THE DOTS to see something magic witches fly on!

FOLLOW THE DOTS to see what takes the children to school!

FOLLOW THE DOTS to see who likes to play tag with the seahorses!

FOLLOW THE DOTS to see what flies in the sky on Halloween!

FOLLOW THE DOTS to see who pulls Santa's sleigh!

FOLLOW THE DOTS to see where spiders live in the haunted house!

FOLLOW THE DOTS to see a spooky fellow!

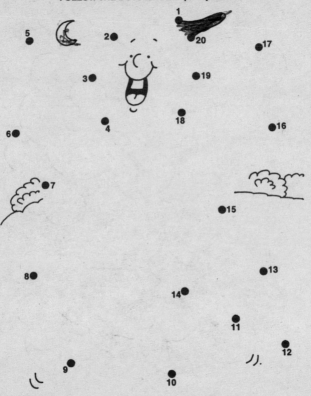

FOLLOW THE DOTS to find out what's in a spooky sky!